Pederson, Charles E.
Jackie Robinson :
baseball great & civil
rights activist

BIO
ROB

DATE DUE

APR 2 8 '71			
MAY 1 2 '71			
OCT 1 3 '71			
JAN 0 6 '72			
JAN 26 '72			
APR 27 '72			

Jackie Robinson: Baseball Great & Civil
Rights Activist
Charles E. Pederson
AR B.L.: 6.6 Alt.: 1005
Points: 2.0   MG

JACKIE ROBINSON

JACKIE ROBINSON

BASEBALL GREAT & CIVIL RIGHTS ACTIVIST

by Charles E. Pederson

Content Consultant:
Hoyt Purvis, Professor of Journalism
University of Arkansas

ABDO
Publishing Company

CREDITS

Published by ABDO Publishing Company, 8000 West 78th Street, Edina, Minnesota 55439. Copyright © 2009 by Abdo Consulting Group, Inc. International copyrights reserved in all countries. No part of this book may be reproduced in any form without written permission from the publisher. The Essential Library™ is a trademark and logo of ABDO Publishing Company.

Printed in the United States.

Editors: Dave McMahon, Holly Saari
Copy Editor: Paula Lewis
Interior Design and Production: Ryan Haugen
Cover Design: Becky Daum

Library of Congress Cataloging-in-Publication Data
Pederson, Charles E.
 Jackie Robinson : baseball great & civil rights activist / by Charles E. Pederson.
    p. cm. — (Essential lives)
 Includes bibliographical references and index.
 ISBN 978-1-60453-526-6
 1. Robinson, Jackie, 1919–1972. 2. African American baseball players—Biography. 3. Baseball players—United States—Biography. 4. Baseball—United States—History. 5. United States—Race relations. I. Title.

 GV865.R6P43 2009
 796.357092—dc22
 [B]

                                  2008033495

TABLE OF CONTENTS

Jackie Robinson broke the color barrier in Major League Baseball on April 15, 1947.

BREAKING THE
COLOR BARRIER

The morning of April 15, 1947, dawned bright, cool, and clear in New York City. It was a day like many early spring days, but it promised to be unlike any other. The players on the Brooklyn professional baseball team, the Dodgers, were dressed in their uniforms and ready to play their opening day game.

Baseball had been called "America's pastime." It seemed to represent the best of the United States. It promoted fair play, encouraged teamwork, and inspired players to do their best and be their best. In the same way baseball displayed the best of the nation, it also showed the worst. Baseball, like much of U.S. society, was segregated. African-American players were not allowed to play in the major leagues.

On that April morning, the players took off their hats. They were honoring the U.S. flag during the playing of "The Star-Spangled Banner." Among them was the first baseman, a rookie. Most rookies started their major league career in their early twenties. At age 28, this player was older than most rookies. Before joining the major leagues, he had played hard, aggressive ball in the Negro leagues.

National Anthem

The song "The Star-Spangled Banner" was written during the War of 1812 by American composer Francis Scott Key. In the morning after one nighttime battle, Key saw the American flag still flying and learned that the city of Baltimore, Maryland, had not surrendered. He quickly wrote a poem to commemorate the effort. The words were later put to music. Congress adopted the song as the U.S. national anthem in 1931. It is usually played before sporting events.

THE "COLOR LINE"

Not only was this man a rookie, but he was also an African American. By playing his first game in the major leagues, he was breaking the "color line." This unwritten rule had kept African Americans out of the major leagues for more than 60 years. The last time an African-American player had played in a Major League Baseball game had been in the 1880s. A catcher, Moses Fleetwood "Fleet" Walker, had briefly played professionally for the Toledo Blue Stockings beginning in 1884.

Walker's follower, 63 years later, was the Dodgers' first baseman, Jackie Robinson. Athletic and competitive, Robinson did not like to lose. He had experience playing with whites during his school athletic career. He had battled racism throughout his life. For those reasons and others, Branch Rickey, the general manager of the Dodgers, had chosen Robinson

Moses Fleetwood Walker

When baseball was first organized, African Americans sometimes played alongside white players. The first African American to play on a major league team was Moses Walker. He was a catcher with the Toledo Blue Stockings. This team joined a major league in 1884. Walker was a highly educated man. He had studied Greek, Latin, German, French, astronomy, botany, geology, and zoology.

to break the color line. Rickey had searched for several years for just the right man. Rickey knew that the player chosen would receive terrible treatment from many people. He needed someone who could control himself, get along with whites, and be an excellent player.

Robinson was ready to prove that an African-American man could play as well as, or better than, any white man. He had promised Rickey that he would not argue or talk back. He promised not to react in any way to the teasing, nasty comments, and ugly behavior he could expect from

Early History of Baseball

Many people believe that Abner Doubleday invented the game of baseball in Cooperstown, New York, in 1839. However, it is clear that the game probably developed from an English game called rounders. Regardless of its origins, by the 1840s, baseball was an organized sport in New York. The first baseball club was the Knickerbockers. The organizer of the team created the field and dimensions that are still used today. He also created a set of rules that remain basically unchanged. The first recorded baseball game took place in Elysian Fields in Hoboken, New Jersey, around 1845.

The U.S. Civil War (1861–1865) helped spread baseball throughout the United States. Many amateur baseball clubs were organized into leagues. The first professional baseball team, the Cincinnati Red Stockings, started in 1868. The team was the first to pay all its players a salary. Seven years later, eight clubs were organized into the National League. In 1901, the American League began, also with eight teams. Several other leagues formed to compete with the National and American leagues, but they failed. The National and American leagues are today's major leagues.

*Branch Rickey talked with players, including Jackie Robinson,
before the 1949 World Series.*

some fans who would not want an African American
playing professional baseball.

On that historic day, Robinson, wearing number
42, stepped across first base. Then he bent down,
resting his hands on his knees. His eyes were serious.
He was ready to play. He wanted to make a good
impression on the fans during his first game. More
importantly, he wanted to succeed for all African
Americans.

A Symbol of Hope

African-American fans flocked to the ball games whenever Robinson played. They supported what many of them saw as a symbol of hope for African Americans in a white world.

Robinson's life had been a series of battles against racism. When Rickey announced he was bringing an African American up to the Dodgers, baseball fans had many different reactions. Robinson had to bear fans who taunted and provoked him and anonymous racists who threatened him and his family. He also faced catchers who spit on his shoes and runners who tried to injure him. He did all this without reacting, although it was a difficult task. Although angry at this treatment, Robinson loved the challenge of being in the big leagues. His sudden rise from minor leaguer to major league player surprised him. He later wrote in his autobiography:

Segregation

Segregation uses law or custom to separate groups. It may be based on race, background, or religion. A more powerful group uses its power to keep another group down. The dominant, or powerful, group expects and usually receives the best jobs, services, or homes.

Next time I go to a movie and see a picture of a little ordinary girl become a great star . . . I'll believe it. And whenever I hear my wife read fairy tales to my little boy, I'll listen. I know now that dreams do come true."[1]

But Jackie Robinson was more than a symbol for equality. He worked hard at playing baseball and ignoring the pressure and conflicts of breaking the color barrier. He paved the way for African-American athletes. Robinson's life after baseball was equally full. During that time he helped pave the way for all Americans to take a step toward respecting one another. ⌒

Brooklyn Baseball Names

The Brooklyn Atlantics were an amateur baseball club organized in 1855. In 1890, the Atlantics changed their nickname to the Bridegrooms. In 1899, the team was sold and the nickname was changed to the Brooklyn Superbas. In 1911, the team name was changed to the Trolley Dodgers. The team's fans had to dodge trolleys (streetcars) on Brooklyn streets. The Trolley Dodgers became the Robins from 1914 until 1931. In 1931, a new manager arrived. The team name was changed back to the Dodgers. The team kept the name Brooklyn Dodgers until it moved to Los Angeles after the 1957 season.

Jackie Robinson, four days before his major league debut

Jim Crow laws allowed waiting rooms and other public facilities to be segregated.

LIFE IN GEORGIA

ackie Robinson had good reason to be aware of racial attitudes in the United States. One set of his grandparents had been slaves before and during the U.S. Civil War (1861–1865). The other set of grandparents had been poor farmers.

Tony Robinson, Jackie's grandfather on his father's side, had lived in Florida. He left the state to rent and farm land on a Georgia plantation owned by Jim Sasser. Tony became a sharecropper on the plantation, which was located near Cairo, Georgia.

Jackie's father, Jerry, grew up on the Sasser plantation. He never learned to read or write. Jackie's mother, Mallie, had a different background. Her parents, Wash and Edna McGriff, had been slaves in Georgia before and during the war. After the Civil War ended, Wash and Edna became freed African Americans. Mallie and her 13 siblings grew up on land her parents owned.

Living in the Jim Crow Era

Although formal slavery had been outlawed, another kind of life began after the Civil War. This period became known as the "Jim Crow" era. The term Jim Crow came from an African-American character in a song from the 1830s. The Jim Crow laws kept African Americans and whites separated. The practices

Juneteenth

The Civil War had been over for two months by the time the people of Galveston, Texas, became aware of it. The day was June 19, quickly shortened to "Juneteenth." It became a sort of second independence day, after the Fourth of July. African Americans celebrated the day more and more widely, until it was known throughout the United States. In 1980, Texas made June 19 an official state holiday, giving state employees the day off. Today, African Americans and people of many other ethnic groups celebrate Juneteenth.

were also called segregation. The Jim Crow era began right after the war during a time called the Reconstruction period.

Sharecropping

Sharecropping began after the U.S. Civil War and was most common in the South. Landowners had fields but little money. Many farmers were poor and had no land of their own. It seemed natural that a barter system would arise. But the practice kept former slaves producing cotton, often on the same land and under the same supervisors.

A sharecropper was a farmer—African-American or white—who lived on land owned by another person. A sharecropper received a certain amount of credit from a landowner. The landowner also provided housing and everything needed to grow a crop. After the crop was harvested, the sharecropper received a share of the profits—sometimes as much as half. The remainder went to the landowner. But the sharecropper also had to repay the credit the landowner had loaned to him. The credit could be much more than the share-cropper's portion of the profits. This resulted in the sharecropper owing more money to the landowner after the harvest. The sharecropper would continue to work for the landowner un-til the debt was paid. Yet it continued to mount with every harvest.

JACKIE'S PARENTS MEET

Wash and Edna McGriff highly valued education and insisted that their children receive as much schooling as possible. They were unhappy when Mallie fell in love with Jerry Robinson, who had no education. Mallie ignored her parents' concerns and in 1909 married Jerry. Soon, the family grew with the birth of their children. Jackie had four older siblings—Edgar (born in 1910), Frank (born in 1911), Mack (born in 1912), and Willa Mae (born in 1916).

Jack Roosevelt Robinson was born on January 31, 1919. His middle name was in honor of former U.S. President Theodore Roosevelt. As president from 1904 to 1911, Roosevelt had spoken strongly against racism and worked hard to help African Americans help themselves.

Mallie and Jerry lived with their family in a house on the Sasser plantation. Jerry worked for Sasser for $12 per month, but the money did not go far enough to feed a growing family. Jerry became bored with farming. He began to spend time away from his home. On July 28, 1919, he left for good. He said he was going to find work in Texas. But in reality, he had moved to the North with a neighbor's wife.

Mallie faced an important decision. She could stay on Sasser's plantation. Or she could pack up her five young children and try to start a new life somewhere else. Her brother Burton lived in

Jim Crow Laws in the South

After African Americans were freed from slavery in 1865 with the passage of the Thirteenth Amendment, they did not receive equal treatment. Segregation and discrimination were widespread. African Americans had to use separate water fountains and phone booths and could not eat in white restaurants. Segregation also contributed to the belief that African Americans should not be allowed to play Major League Baseball.

Pasadena, California. He had invited her more than once to move there. She decided it was time to leave. She began to look to the West and to California. ⌐

President Roosevelt

Theodore Roosevelt was vice president when U.S. President William McKinley was assassinated. Roosevelt was 42 when he became the nation's youngest president. He was well-known as an energetic, youthful president. He had lived as a hunter, cowboy, and military leader. He vigorously promoted U.S. interests around the world, including construction of the Panama Canal. He was also a strong conservationist. He established five new national parks and added hundreds of millions of protected acres to national forests. He once said, "I do not believe that anyone else has ever enjoyed the White House as much as I have."[1]

Jackie Robinson's middle name honored President Theodore Roosevelt.

The Robinsons experienced challenges and opportunities in Pasadena, California.

CALIFORNIA AND ITS CHALLENGES

On May 22, 1920, the Robinsons left Georgia. Mallie and her children took the train from Cairo, Georgia, and headed for Pasadena, California. Little Jackie was 16 months old. Once the Robinsons arrived, they moved into a small house with their extended family. This included Uncle Burton and the Wades, Mallie's sister and her husband.

AT HOME ON PEPPER STREET

By 1922, Mallie was ready to move her family again. She and the Wades put their money together. They bought a home at 121 Pepper Street in Pasadena. The large, two-story house had five bedrooms and two bathrooms. A vegetable garden and fruit trees provided food for the Robinsons. Mallie also raised chickens and other animals. The house became Jackie's home until he left 19 years later.

At the end of World War I (1914–1918), many whites that had served overseas in the military returned to Pasadena. They needed jobs and houses. This provided a conflict with the African Americans who had stayed in Pasadena. As a

Pasadena "Golden Age"

The early 1900s were a "golden age" for African Americans in Pasadena. By the 1920s, Pasadena was one of the richest U.S. cities. Many African Americans had moved to Pasadena from southern states. Its rapid growth opened many jobs that African Americans filled. Wealthy whites that lived in Pasadena hired African Americans as household servants and other workers.

result, the white and African-American populations in Pasadena became segregated. Jackie once said, "People in Pasadena were less understanding, in some ways, than southerners. And they were more openly hostile."[1]

The Robinson family experienced this firsthand. Many white neighbors did not welcome them. Some of the angry neighbors tried to buy the house from Mallie and the Wades. At one point, a cross was burned on their front lawn. A burning cross was a symbol of racial violence and intimidation. A white supremacy organization called

Jackie's Siblings

Jackie's siblings influenced him greatly. Of his oldest brother, Edgar, Jackie confessed, "There was always something about him that was mysterious to me."[2] Edgar had little education but could quote the Bible at will. He also enjoyed speed—especially on bikes, roller skates, or motorcycles.

Frank was gentle and outgoing. He "was my greatest fan," said Jackie.[3] Jim Crow laws in Pasadena had taken away Frank's job. He and his family lived with Mallie.

Because Mallie worked, Jackie's sister, Willa Mae, cared for Jackie when he was growing up. She fed and dressed him. In kindergarten, she could not watch him directly. Teachers let him play in the sandbox as Willa Mae kept an eye on him from her desk. At the end of the day, she brought him back home.

Athletically, Jackie was most like his brother Mack. A speedy track star in high school and college, Mack won a spot on the 1936 summer Olympics team, in Berlin, Germany. He placed second in the 200-meter dash, losing to Jesse Owens. This was no small accomplishment, considering that Owens won four gold medals in the Olympics that year.

the Ku Klux Klan often burned crosses this way to frighten African Americans. Other neighbors signed a petition to try to force the Robinsons and Wades out of their home. However, they refused to sell or give in to the pressure.

Mallie was a proud, dignified, and self-assured woman. She would not take insults from her neighbors, but she also refused to get even with them. Instead, she treated them kindly. She taught her children the value and importance of respect.

Mallie also wanted to pass on to her children her love of God. She brought her children to the Scott United Methodist Church every Sunday. Arnold Rampersad wrote in *Jackie Robinson: A Biography*, "Through all his years living with Mallie, Jack was witness to his mother's unshakable attachment to religion."[4]

Exclusion Acts

African Americans were not the only group that faced discrimination in California. The state had a history of prejudice against Chinese and Japanese immigrants. During the California Gold Rush of 1848, large numbers of Chinese came to the United States. They were accepted at first, but during an economic slowdown, whites pointed at Chinese immigrants as part of the cause. As a result, Congress passed laws, called exclusion acts, to keep more Chinese from immigrating to the United States. The laws were later extended to cover Japanese immigrants too. The laws were not repealed until 1965.

Jackie Starts School

Mallie made sure that Jackie, along with his brothers and sister, went to school. In junior high, Jackie began to blossom as an athlete and excelled at all the sports he tried. A longtime friend, Ray Bartlett, said Jackie "always played his best and did his best and gave all he had, and he didn't like to lose."[5]

Jackie also grew more independent and joined the Pepper Street Gang. Although the gang did not take part in violent crimes, it did partake in mischief. Jackie did not have a father at home and sought a male adult to guide him. Carl Anderson, a mechanic in the area where the Pepper Street Gang operated, stepped into that role. Anderson took Jackie aside and told him that he did not belong in a gang. He told Jackie that having inner strength meant not following a gang. It took real inner strength to

Scott United Methodist Church

Mallie Robinson's church was part of a larger group called the United Methodist Church. Located only a short distance from the Rose Bowl football stadium, Scott Methodist was founded in 1903. Bishop Isaiah Scott started the church, which met in various members' homes until 1930. That year, the church building was constructed. In September 2003, the church celebrated its one hundredth anniversary.

be different. He pointed out that Jackie was hurting not only himself but also his mother. Jackie took the advice to heart and later wrote, "I was too ashamed to tell Carl how right he was, but what he said got to me."[6]

After his brief period in the Pepper Street Gang ended, Jackie focused on athletics. Jackie finished his high school career in spectacular style. During his time at John Muir Technical High School, his athletic ability continued to improve. He was a very good shortstop for the baseball team and later played catcher. He was a leader on the basketball team and helped the team win the 1937 season championship. In track, he competed in the broad jump and pole vault. On the football team, Jackie was a star quarterback. He won the junior boys' singles tournament in the Pacific Coast Negro Tennis Tournament. His desire to win and his self-discipline appeared in every part of his life. Friends often commented on the self-discipline he displayed on and off the field.

Jackie's athletic ability showed him a world where whites and African Americans could compete equally and still respect each other. After experiencing this, Arnold Rampersad wrote, "nothing could convince Robinson that Jim Crow in any sport—or in any other aspect of American life, for that matter—was right or natural."[7] He carried these beliefs through his youth and into adulthood. They would influence him throughout his baseball career and his life afterward.

Jesse Owens and the 1936 Olympics

Adolf Hitler and his Nazi political party believed the white race was better than all others. During the 1936 Olympics, they hoped to prove it to the world. However, a U.S. athlete named Jesse Owens disproved their theory. Born in Alabama, Owens became a world-class sprinter. He gained a spot on the U.S. Olympic team. He won four sprints at the Olympics, defeating the German athletes, as well as all others. Owens was called "the world's fastest human."[8] However, even after the stunning victories, Owens had to live in a segregated United States.

Jesse Owens competed in the 200-meter dash in the 1936 Summer Olympics.

Jackie Robinson was an important player on the UCLA football team.

GROWING UP AND GETTING OUT

After Jackie graduated from John Muir Technical High School, he enrolled in Pasadena Junior College. His brother Mack was also enrolled at the school, and the two kept up a fierce track-and-field competition.

Jackie was an outstanding football player. He joined the Pasadena Junior College team, the Bulldogs. Some of the other Bulldogs were southerners. They treated Jackie and the other African Americans poorly. It is not clear whether Jackie confronted the players or went to the coach, but he threatened to transfer to a different school. Whatever the case, the coach put a stop to the poor treatment. From that, "Jack learned a lesson both about the value of protesting injustice and about using his market value as an athlete to fight against it."[1]

A MULTISPORT ATHLETE

Robinson also played basketball and baseball for Pasadena Junior College. As a baseball player, Robinson developed the energetic, aggressive play that he displayed later in the major leagues. He led the league in most categories and

Mack Robinson

Jackie's older brother Mack was an excellent broad jumper at Pasadena Junior College. He set a college broad jump record that Jackie later broke. Mack attended the college mainly to train for track. Jackie and Mack competed against each other in the broad jump. Jackie lost every time until late in his freshman year. Mack's accomplishments in the 1936 Olympics were a high point in his life. When he returned home after a tour of Europe, life was ordinary. He never finished his college education. Instead, he took a street-sweeping job in Pasadena. Mack died in 2000 at age 88.

earned the praise of many people. Most players as good as he was would have been courted by a Major League Baseball team. But as an African American, Robinson could not play in the majors. As a major league manager put it, "If that kid [Jack] was white I'd sign him right now."[2]

While at Pasadena Junior College, Robinson matured and became more self-assured and outgoing. He also met Jack Gordon, who became one of his lifelong friends. During this time, another friend stepped into Robinson's life. Karl Downs, the pastor at Robinson's home church, listened to Robinson's problems and interested him in teaching Sunday school classes. From this, Robinson's faith in God became increasingly important in his life.

ARREST BRINGS QUESTIONS OF RACISM

Robinson could not escape racism in Pasadena. In September 1939, Robinson and some friends were riding in a car when a white driver in another car cut them off. The man got out of the car as though he wanted to fight. Robinson confronted the man, who decided to leave. At that moment, a police officer arrived. Refusing to be intimidated, Robinson was arrested at gunpoint. He spent the night in jail before University of California at Los Angeles (UCLA) officials, who coveted his athletic talents, arranged for Robinson's release and a suspended sentence. Robinson's athletic talent attracted many four-year colleges nationwide. Because he wanted to stay close to home, he accepted a scholarship from UCLA.

Robinson was able to relax the summer before beginning classes at UCLA. He won the singles and doubles divisions of the Western Federation of Tennis Clubs tournament for African Americans. He also helped the Pasadena Sox, a mixed-race baseball team, win the California State Amateur Baseball

Pasadena Junior College

Pasadena Junior College grew out of Pasadena High School, which was established in 1911. The college opened on the high school property in 1924. It served as grades 13 and 14 of Pasadena High School. The college grew steadily through the years. In 1954 it merged with John Muir Junior College and became Pasadena City College (PCC). Today, PCC offers 60 programs for more than 25,000 students every year.

championship. Beyond that, these months were the first time in years that Jackie was not training for a sport.

In the fall of 1939, Robinson began classes. He told UCLA that he was going to concentrate only on football and the broad jump, instead of his usual four or five sports. Robinson trained hard in the broad jump and hoped to follow Mack to win a place on the U.S. Olympic team. When World War II began, the 1940 Olympics were cancelled, and Robinson's hopes ended. Along with football and track, he again took up basketball and baseball. He continued to excel in these sports. After the baseball season, Robinson continued training for the broad jump. He won a national collegiate title and set a conference record. He had already lettered that year in his three other sports, and now he also lettered in track. He became the first UCLA student to letter in four sports in one year.

Robinson Meets His College Sweetheart

One of the most important events of Robinson's life occurred in 1940, when he was a senior. His friend Ray Bartlett introduced Robinson to Rachel Isum, a freshman nursing student. Jackie later said,

Robinson met his future wife, Rachel Isum, at UCLA.

"From the beginning I realized there was something very special about Rae."[4]

Rachel's father did not like her past boyfriends very much, and Robinson was no exception. Rachel's mother, however, liked Robinson immediately. He was everything she had hoped for in a partner for Rachel. He was gentle, serious, religious, and good-looking.

In 1940, Rachel's father died. Her deep sadness made Robinson realize how much he loved her. He commented, "In this time of sorrow we found each other and I knew then that our relationship was to be one of the most important things in my life."[5]

By 1941, Robinson had been named best all-around athlete on the West Coast. He led the Pacific Coast Conference in basketball scoring. He won the Pacific Coast Intercollegiate Golf Championship. He also reached the semifinals of the National Negro Tennis Tournament. His legend as an athlete was firmly grounded in fact.

However, his mother faced financial burdens at home, and Robinson dropped out of school to help her. Rachel strongly believed he should graduate. Robinson disagreed. He believed that "no amount of education would help a black man get a job."[6]

Robinson's first job was as an athletic director for the National Youth Administration (NYA). A government-supported program, the NYA helped young people find jobs. Robinson's new job combined his deep desires to help kids and to help his mother. Most of the kids Robinson supervised where white, but he noticed how "the color of his skin didn't seem to matter" to them.[7] The job lasted only a few months. The military draft took over the NYA's role of finding work for young people, and Robinson was let go.

With the loss of his first job, Robinson returned to playing sports. This time he looked for a professional sport to help him earn money. Major league sports still did not allow African-American players. The only team that offered Robinson a job was a football team, the Honolulu Bears. It was only a minor league team, but it was integrated. Robinson moved to Hawaii to play for the team. He played football on Sundays. During the rest of the

Pearl Harbor

During World War II, the United States was determined not to enter the war. It did not take military action against Germany or Japan as the two countries took over many of their neighboring territories. Instead, the United States quit sending products to Japan. This frightened Japan's leaders, who saw the United States as the only power that could stop them from expanding even more. They planned an attack to destroy the U.S. Navy's Pacific fleet.

Before sunrise on December 7, 1941, a Japanese naval fleet approached Pearl Harbor on the Hawaiian island of Oahu. Aircraft carriers in the Japanese fleet launched more than 300 airplanes early in the day. They bombed and shot at as many U.S. aircraft parked on airfields and at as many ships as they could. The attack killed more than 2,000 people at Pearl Harbor, wounding approximately 2,000 more. The Japanese airplanes ruined or damaged 21 American ships and more than 300 planes. The Japanese lost only 29 aircraft. The next day, the U.S. Congress declared war on Japan. The attack on Pearl Harbor brought U.S. troops into World War II. On August 14, 1945, Japan surrendered.

National Youth Administration

In June 1935, President Franklin Roosevelt signed into law the National Youth Administration (NYA). The NYA was created to provide jobs for young people affected by the Great Depression. It had two purposes. First, it provided educational money in return for students' work. It also provided on-the-job training so young people would have skills they could use in the future. By 1943, the Great Depression had ended. The need to provide this type of job training for young people had passed. Funding was not renewed to continue the program.

week, he worked for a construction company near Pearl Harbor.

After the season ended, Robinson wanted to return to Pasadena. He boarded a ship for California on December 5, 1941. On December 7, 1941, Japanese aircraft bombed the U.S. Navy base at Pearl Harbor. This attack drew the United States into World War II. Robinson was playing cards on board a ship with some other men when the news reached them about the bombing. Robinson began to consider the real possibility that he might have to enter the military.

The National Youth Administration's mostly white participants looked beyond Jackie Robinson's skin color.

Jackie Robinson, left, and boxer Joe Louis, right, served in the army together.

ENTERING A WORLD
AT WAR

On March 23, 1942, Robinson received a letter from the U.S. government. It told him to report for army duty on April 3. He was sent for basic training to Fort Riley, Kansas. Robinson, along with other African Americans, applied to

Officer Candidate School (OCS). In OCS, soldiers learned how to be army leaders.

Robinson was an excellent candidate for OCS. He was an expert marksman, and his character was rated as excellent. His four years of college, his self-discipline, and his intelligence should have immediately placed him in OCS. But Robinson endured several months of waiting. He and other African Americans were refused entry while less-qualified white applicants were accepted. The army seemed to believe that African Americans did not have the ability to lead other men.

MEETING A BOXING LEGEND

Soon after Robinson entered the army, Joe Louis was assigned to Fort Riley for basic training. Louis was a world famous African-American boxer. In 1938, he had beaten the German boxing champion in another blow against Nazi racism. Before long, Robinson and Louis were good friends. Louis heard about Robinson's and the others' delay in being accepted into OCS. He made

Joe Louis

Joe Louis, nicknamed the Brown Bomber, was possibly the best boxer in U.S. history. Born in 1914, in Lafayette, Alabama, he began boxing at a young age. At age 18, he turned professional. In 1937, he defeated the heavyweight boxing champion to become the champion. From 1937 to 1949, he successfully defended his championship 25 times.

some calls to powerful friends. It is not clear whether his calls had an effect or whether Robinson was already in process to enter OCS. But both men were accepted into OCS. On January 28, 1943, Robinson became a second lieutenant in the army.

OCS was integrated, with whites and African Americans working, living, and studying side by side. Many other areas of the army, however, were still segregated. This included army sports. Robinson wanted to play on the Fort Riley baseball team. He learned that blacks were not welcome. Pete Reiser, who later played with Robinson for the Dodgers, was on the Fort Riley team. On Robinson's attempt to join the team, Reiser recalled:

> *A Negro lieutenant [Robinson] came out for the team. An officer told him "You have to play with the colored team."... There was no colored team. The black lieutenant didn't speak. He stood there for a while, watched us work out, and then he turned and walked away.... That was the first time I saw Jackie Robinson.[1]*

Robinson joined the base's football team. The first game was scheduled against the University of Missouri. The university team members complained about Robinson. They said they would not play against African Americans. Instead of telling Robinson the real reason, the army said Robinson should visit home. When he learned the army made the offer to keep him out of the game against the University of Missouri, Robinson quit the team.

LENDING A HAND TO OTHERS

Robinson became the unofficial morale officer for African Americans. Soldiers came to him for guidance and advice. He saw more examples of Jim Crow laws. Soldiers complained that not enough seating was available for African Americans in the base cafeteria. Robinson called the officer in charge to ask for more spaces. The officer did not know Robinson

Desegregation of the Military

The U.S. military had a long history of segregation, which began during the Civil War. After the Emancipation Proclamation, the U.S. Army began accepting African Americans. Most of them did not fight, however. Instead, they supported white soldiers as cooks and laborers. African Americans did fight during World War II and after—but not alongside whites.

By 1946, President Harry Truman began working toward desegregating the military. Truman realized that, politically, it would be good to work for civil rights. In November 1947, the Committee Against Jim Crow in Military Service and Training was established.

On July 26, 1948, Truman signed Executive Order 9981 to end racial discrimination in the military. Despite the order, some officers and others were slow to end discrimination. Finally, during the Korean War (1950–1953), the army announced it was formally ending segregation and discrimination.

was African-American, and he insulted African Americans. His comments made Robinson so angry that he ended up shouting at the officer.

Robinson reported the conversation to his commander, Colonel Longley. The colonel said "that he would write a letter to the commanding general asking that conditions at the post exchange be corrected."[2] Later, more seats were assigned to African-American soldiers.

Robinson Arrested at Military Base

In April 1944, Robinson and other African-American officers were sent to Fort Hood, Texas. Robinson's unit worked very hard there and received an excellent rating.

Jim Crow laws at Fort Riley were bad, but at Fort Hood it was much worse. Part of southern life included making African Americans sit at the back of buses. The best seats, near the front, were saved for white passengers. Texas buses were no different, and Robinson obeyed the law when he rode city buses.

The army announced that military buses, however, were not to be segregated. On July 6, Robinson rode a military bus to the hospital in a nearby town to have his ankle examined.

Robinson was aware that military buses were not to be segregated. He not only refused to sit at the back of the bus when ordered to, but he also argued with the driver. At the base's central station, the driver had someone call the base police. Robinson was arrested. He was to be court-martialed for disobeying orders. A court-martial is a trial in a military court.

The court-martial was not for several months. During that time, he visited Rachel. She was not sure anymore whether she should be with Robinson. She worried that marriage would cut short her nursing career. Robinson was hurt and confused, and the two stopped seeing each other. During this time, Karl Downs, who had moved to Austin, Texas, counseled Robinson.

Robinson's court-martial took place on August 2, 1944. The prosecution tried to frame Robinson unfairly. But after four hours, all charges were dropped. However, the trial had caused him to miss going to

Military Justice

All branches of the armed forces follow a system of laws called the Uniform Code of Military Justice. Created by Congress in 1951, the code describes conduct considered criminal. Most of this conduct is similar to nonmilitary crimes. The code also covers military conduct such as disobeying an officer. In most ways, a court-martial, which follows the rules of the code, is similar to a nonmilitary trial. The main difference is that a court-martial has no jury. Instead, officers serve as judges and vote on the case. Two-thirds or three-fourths of the officers, depending on the case, must agree on a ruling. If the death penalty is recommended, all the judges must agree.

The Tuskegee Airmen

During World War II, the army was still racially segregated. However, under pressure, it did agree that African-American men could begin to train as pilots for the Army Air Corps. (The Army Air Corps later became the U.S. Air Force.) They trained at the Tuskegee Institute, a college founded by Booker T. Washington, a former slave. The Tuskegee pilots, crewmen, and ground support men became highly respected for their performances in North Africa and Europe. One of the first Tuskegee pilots to earn his wings was Benjamin O. Davis Jr. He later became the first African-American general in the air force.

Europe with his unit. He requested an honorable discharge and received it on November 28, 1944.

Robinson's time in the army was frustrating. Jim Crow laws had kept him and many other African Americans from advancing. However, as his biographer Arnold Rampersad commented, "He was far more deeply invested now in a personal commitment to the ideal of social justice, especially for blacks."[3]

*The Tuskegee Airmen became the first African-American
fighting squadron in the army.*

*Kansas City Monarchs pitcher Satchel Paige was a sensation
in the Negro leagues.*

THE
NEGRO LEAGUES

After leaving the army, Robinson began
to look for work. A friend suggested
that he try out with the Kansas City Monarchs. The
Monarchs were part of baseball's Negro leagues and
featured the great pitcher Leroy "Satchel" Paige.

Kept from the major leagues for 60 years, African Americans had formed their own professional league.

Many people wondered why African Americans had been banned. "No rule in organized baseball" kept them out, according to Judge Kenesaw Mountain Landis, the baseball commissioner.[1] The main reason for not allowing African Americans to play in the major leagues was because white players would not play with them.

ROBINSON QUESTIONS HIS PLAYING CAREER

Robinson earned $400 per month with the Monarchs. Still, the Negro leagues did not impress Robinson. He disliked them because the leagues were segregated. Robinson was against all forms of segregation, even those that African Americans introduced. He would have preferred that African

Satchel Paige

Leroy "Satchel" Paige was a star pitcher for the Kansas City Monarchs during the 1945 season that Robinson spent with the team. Paige was one of the most popular players in the Negro Leagues and one of its best pitchers. In one exhibition game, he struck out 21 major league batters. In 1948, he joined the Cleveland Indians as the American League's first African-American pitcher. Joe DiMaggio, a legendary hitter for the New York Yankees, said Paige was the greatest pitcher he ever faced.

Kenesaw Mountain Landis

In 1919, the Chicago "Black Sox" scandal rocked Major League Baseball. Eight Chicago White Sox players were accused of taking money from gamblers to let the Cincinnati Reds win the World Series. Worried that disgusted fans would stay away from games, the team owners hired a commissioner to improve and protect baseball's reputation. They chose Kenesaw Mountain Landis, a U.S. district court judge. One of his first acts was to ban the eight "Black Sox" players. He made other changes that rebuilt baseball's reputation for fair play. Landis acted as commissioner until his death in 1944.

Americans and whites play together. He even questioned whether he should continue playing baseball and remarked, "I began to wonder why I should dedicate my life to a career where the boundaries for progress were set by racial discrimination."[2]

The travel was tiring, and the Jim Crow living conditions disgusted Robinson, who wrote:

Finding satisfactory or even passable eating places was almost a daily problem. There was no hotel in many of the places we played. Sometimes there was a hotel for blacks which had no eating facilities. No one even thought of trying to get accommodations in white hotels. Some of the crummy eating joints would not serve us at all. You could never sit down to a relaxed hot meal. You were lucky if they magnanimously permitted you to carry out some greasy hamburgers in a paper bag with a container of coffee.[3]

Branch Rickey Develops a Plan

Branch Rickey, the general manager of the Brooklyn Dodgers Major League Baseball team, stepped into the situation and developed a plan. By 1943, he saw a need for new players to fill the spaces left by white players who were at war. After years as general manager in St. Louis, Rickey was finally in a position where he could carry out a plan. First, he increased scouting of new players nationwide. Then, he proposed that if a scout saw any African-American players who were good enough for the majors, they should be signed. Other Dodgers administrators agreed.

In explaining why he wanted to introduce African Americans to the major leagues, he often claimed that he simply saw a way to earn money. But different statements hinted at other reasons. He also repeated the following story. He was a young coach for the Ohio Wesleyan University baseball team. The team's only African American, Charles Thomas, had been barred from the hotel where the white players stayed. When Rickey strongly protested, Thomas was allowed to share Rickey's room. At one point, Rickey found Thomas sobbing and rubbing at his skin, saying, "Black skin! If I could only make [it] white."[4]

*Branch Rickey was intent on signing Robinson as the first
African American in the major leagues.*

Rickey later said, "That scene haunted me for many
years."[5]

Rickey publicly stated that he wanted to start
a new Negro league team, the Brooklyn Brown
Dodgers. They would use Ebbets Field in Brooklyn
when the Dodgers played away games. However, he
used the Brown Dodgers as a screen. By claiming to
scout African Americans for his Negro leagues team,
he could secretly look for talented players who could

be in the major leagues. Rickey's scouts for the Dodgers fanned out across the United States. Several scouts reported seeing Robinson play during the 1945 Monarchs season. They told Rickey that Robinson's all-around play was excellent.

Robinson had no idea major league scouts were watching him. But he did have an idea that he was ready to quit the Kansas City Monarchs. He was going to make one last barnstorming tour to earn some money. Then he intended to marry Rachel and settle down near Los Angeles. Rachel had graduated from nursing school and was working at Los Angeles General Hospital.

Finally, head scout Clyde Sukeforth went to see Robinson. Sukeforth knew only that Rickey was interested in Robinson for the Brown Dodgers. Rickey was willing to meet Robinson in Los Angeles if Robinson would not meet him in New York.

Jackie's First Professional Tryout

On April 16, 1945, Robinson and two other African Americans had a major league tryout with the Boston Red Sox. Robinson's play was excellent. The chief Boston scout, Hugh Duffy, said, "What a ballplayer! Too bad he's the wrong color."[6] Nothing came of the tryout, just as Robinson had expected. In fact, almost no one from the Red Sox showed up to see the players.

On August 28, 1945, Robinson traveled to
Brooklyn to meet Rickey and Sukeforth at the
Dodgers' headquarters. There, Rickey revealed his
true purpose. He did not want Robinson for the
Brown Dodgers. He wanted Robinson to play for the
Dodgers' major league team.

Rickey saw Robinson's talent, but he believed
many African Americans could play well. What he
really needed was the most "suitable" player. Rickey
later recalled he had to "be sure that the man was
good on the field, (but more important that he was
not) the wrong man off the field."[7]

Rickey was pleased to hear that Robinson had
Rachel in his life. He believed Robinson would need
a partner to help handle the challenges he foresaw.

MAKING A COMMITMENT TO RICKEY

Rickey tried to show Robinson what he thought
would happen if Robinson joined the major leagues.
Rickey played the parts of many different types of
bigots. He shouted racial insults. He asked how
Robinson would handle being attacked or refused
food or a hotel room because of his skin color.

After three hours, Rickey's main point was clear.
Rickey said, "Robinson, I'm looking for a ballplayer

with guts enough not to fight back."[8] Robinson had to promise not to react to any of the abuse people threw at him. He could never argue—on or off the field.

Robinson was skeptical of the promises. But Rickey seemed different. Arnold Rampersad wrote, "In their relatively brief meeting, Rickey had probably shown more concentrated personal fury and passion on the question of race and sports than Jack had ever seen in a white man."[9] Robinson accepted the offer.

Rickey wanted to sign Robinson to play with the Montreal Royals, which was part of the Brooklyn

The Baseball Farm System

Most people consider Branch Rickey to be the inventor of the farm system in baseball. In 1921, Rickey was general manager of the St. Louis Cardinals. He worried about major league teams stealing talent from other teams by offering players more money. Rickey decided to buy minor league teams. The teams in this system are called farm teams. They are part of the farm system. There are many minor leagues nationwide, but only some of those teams are part of the farm system. The farm players grow and mature in skills, much as crops grow and mature on a farm.

Farm teams are now ranked as A, AA, or AAA clubs. Currently, AAA is the most advanced rating for a farm team. Major league teams put farm players under contract and let them play in the minor leagues. Signing a contract means the players agree to play for only the teams in the major league club's system. The players who perform best in the minor leagues will move up in the farm system and may get called up to play in the major leagues.

The Montreal Royals

The French-speaking Canadian city of Montreal has a long baseball history. A minor league team first formed there in 1890. The Montreal team joined various leagues over the years until becoming part of the International League in 1928. In 1939, the Brooklyn Dodgers bought the team, which became a AAA club. This was the last stop for rising players before reaching the majors. Robinson helped propel the club to the league championship. In 1960, the team quit being a Brooklyn farm team. Professional baseball returned to Montreal in 1969, when the Expos joined the National League. However, in 2005 the team moved to Washington DC and became the Nationals.

farm system. He would receive $3,500 for signing the contract. His salary would be $600 per month. Robinson signed the contract on October 23, 1945. He had taken the first step to breaking the color barrier.

Robinson signed his contract for Major League Baseball on April 10, 1947.

Robinson played his first season in the minor leagues with the Montreal Royals.

In the Minors

On February 10, 1946, the Reverend Karl Downs married Robinson and Rachel in a large wedding at the Independent Church of Christ in Los Angeles. Shortly after their wedding, the couple began the trip from Los Angeles to Daytona

Beach, Florida. Robinson was to report there for spring training with the Montreal Royals. Unfortunately, Jim Crow laws began to appear on the trip to Florida.

During a layover in New Orleans, they were asked to leave the plane. The airline representatives gave them several reasons, none of which made sense. Then, when the couple looked for a restaurant, none would serve them. Their airplane seats continued to be given to whites. They had to wait 12 hours for a flight out of New Orleans.

When the plane landed in Pensacola, Florida, Robinson and Rachel were again bumped from their seats so whites could fly. The couple found a bus to Daytona Beach, but they had to sit in the Jim Crow section at the back. Robinson was angry, but later wrote, "I had no right to lose my temper and jeopardize the chances of all the blacks who would

Karl Downs

Karl Downs played an important part in Robinson's life long after Downs had left Pasadena. Downs moved to Austin, Texas. He became president of Samuel Huston College, which was affiliated with the Methodist church. In 1945, Downs hired Robinson briefly as a physical education teacher. He also performed the 1946 marriage ceremony of Robinson and Rachel. Downs died in late February 1948.

follow me if I could help break down the barriers."[1]

Finally, the Robinsons made it to Daytona Beach. Compared to much of the rest of the South, the city was welcoming to Robinson and another African American, John Wright, a pitcher that Rickey signed. Although the Robinsons, Wright, and other African Americans could not stay in the same hotel with the white players, at least the town officially welcomed them. In practice, they remained alone and lonely.

Outside Daytona Beach, Jackie and Rachel were often threatened and ridiculed. At one stadium, the gates were padlocked when the Royals arrived. At another, the team claimed that the ball field lights were not working, although Robinson wondered what that had to do "with the fact that the game was to be played in the daytime."[2]

Branch Rickey Stands Up for Robinson

Poor treatment of Robinson by other teams and fans was as bad as Branch Rickey imagined it would be. Some teams vowed not to play the Dodgers if Robinson was going to play. When that happened, Rickey threatened to cancel the games.

Jackie Robinson scrambled safely back to first base after a pickoff attempt.

A ROUGH START ON THE FIELD

Early in the preseason, Robinson injured his arm and had to miss several games. He also had a hitting slump. Arnold Rampersad commented, "To many blacks, watching Robinson struggle was deeply upsetting; they felt their race's suffering in his ordeal."[3]

April 18, 1946, was the Royals' opening day, and Robinson was the starting second baseman. In his first at bat, Robinson grounded out. In his second time up, Robinson hit a three-run home run. He ended his first game in the minor leagues with four hits, including the home run. He also stole second base twice and scored four times. The Montreal Royals won the game 14–1.

FEELING AT HOME IN CANADA

Jackie and Rachel rented a small apartment in Montreal for the regular season. After the poor behavior of white fans in the United States, the couple was surprised at the kind treatment of white Canadians. They made friends with some of their neighbors, even though the couple spoke no French, the language of most of their neighbors. The two looked back on their time in Montreal with great fondness.

The Royals ended the season by winning the 1946 Little World Series, which was played by the champions of the International League and

A Sports Trailblazer

Robinson helped pave the way for African Americans in other sports, too. On March 21, 1946, Kenny Washington became the first African American to sign with a professional football team. He played the position of quarterback. Without Robinson's leadership in baseball, it might have been many more years before an African American could play professional football.

the American Association, another AAA league. Robinson's .349 batting average and 113 runs led the International League. He had the best fielding percentage in the league. At the end of the series, Robinson's manager, Clay Hopper, shook his hand and said how glad he was to have had him on his team. Only later did Robinson learn that Hopper had begged Rickey not to send Robinson to his team.

After the last game of the Little World Series, the Montreal fans stormed the field when Robinson returned to it. They shook his hand, lifted him in the air, and carried him around, singing victory songs. Sportswriter

Barnstorming Tours

Barnstorming consisted of traveling to different cities and playing exhibition games during the off-season. Nearly all Negro league players took part in barnstorming. One main reason for the off-season games was to earn additional money. Many players found it difficult to survive on their meager baseball salaries. Barnstorming allowed them to bring in more money by continuing to do what they loved.

Barnstorming was also a chance to entertain spectators and prove how talented Negro leaguers truly were. Often, Negro league teams would play major league teams. It was a chance for them to show white fans what good players they were.

Yet, barnstorming was also difficult and tiring. Players would travel all across the country—Kansas City, St. Louis, Toledo, Chicago, and Pittsburgh. They usually traveled by bus. Players often slept and ate on the bus because hotels and restaurants might not serve them. Robinson made several barnstorming tours that took him throughout the United States and into Central and South America.

Sam Maltin wrote, "It was probably the only day in history that a black man ran from a white mob with love instead of lynching on its mind."[4]

After a barnstorming tour, Robinson returned to Los Angeles with Rachel. She had become pregnant during the season. On November 18, 1946, Robinson was at the hospital when Rachel delivered their first child, Jack Roosevelt Robinson Jr.

Clay Hopper

Montreal manager Clay Hopper, a native of Mississippi, held racist ideas toward African Americans. Robinson was no exception for him. At one game, Branch Rickey stood next to Hopper. Rickey commented that a play Robinson made was "superhuman." Hopper turned to Rickey and wondered whether he seriously thought African Americans were humans. By the end of the season, however, Hopper's attitude toward Robinson had changed. He called him a gentleman and told the press that Robinson definitely should be in the major leagues.

*A Royals teammate congratulated Jackie Robinson
after he hit a home run against the Jersey City Giants.*

Leo Durocher was an advocate for Jackie Robinson playing in the major leagues.

BREAKING INTO THE MAJORS

Spring training rolled around again for the Montreal Royals in 1947. The Dodgers had signed three other African-American players to play with the Royals. Pitchers Don Newcombe and Roy Partlow and catcher Roy Campanella joined

the team. Rickey moved spring training for both the
Royals and the Dodgers to Havana, Cuba. He hoped
to avoid the racist problems of Florida.

The Cuban fans strongly supported Robinson
and the others. But the African-American players
were still not allowed to share the same hotel as
the white players. It seemed to Robinson that he
could not escape Jim Crow laws anywhere he went.
Rickey told Robinson the separate accommodations
had been his idea. He was worried that white U.S.
tourists might be upset to share a hotel with African
Americans. He felt the success of having an African
American in the major leagues was near, and he
did not want anything to mess it up. Robinson
reluctantly accepted the situation.

The Dodgers and the Royals played training
games against each other. Robinson played
incredibly well. But still, the question everyone was
asking remained: Would Rickey promote Robinson
to the Dodgers or leave him with Montreal for
another season?

Durocher Wants Robinson on the Dodgers

The players on the Dodgers had the same
question. Several southern players circulated a

petition to keep him out. Not all the players signed the petition, not even all the southern players. Some who did, however, were traded before the season began. The manager, Leo Durocher, told his players that they better not try to keep Robinson off the team. Rickey firmly expressed his feelings as well: "No player on this club will have anything to say about who plays or does not play on it. I will decide who is on it and Durocher will decide who . . . does the playing."[1]

Robinson Handed No. 42

It was April 10, 1947, less than a week before the start of the major league season. The Royals and the Dodgers were playing an exhibition game against each other. Rickey's assistant handed a typewritten announcement to the press at the game: "The Brooklyn Dodgers today purchased the contract of Jackie Roosevelt Robinson from the

Durocher Is Suspended

As a player in the major leagues, Leo "the Lip" Durocher was famous for his back talk. He argued with everybody, from umpires to fans. As the Dodgers manager, he continued arguing. Before Robinson was brought up to the Dodgers, baseball commissioner Albert "Happy" Chandler suspended Durocher from managing for allegedly consorting with known gamblers. Newspapers covered the standoff between the two men. Durocher's publicity helped relieve some of the pressure that might have fallen on Robinson. It made his entry into the major leagues a little easier.

Montreal Royals. He will report immediately [to play with the Dodgers]. Signed, Branch Rickey."[2]

When Robinson arrived in Brooklyn, Clyde Sukeforth was there to hand him his uniform, number 42. He told Robinson he would play first base in an exhibition series against the New York Yankees. Robinson was officially a Major League Baseball player.

Rickey was concerned not only about whites' reactions to Robinson's entering the majors. He was also equally concerned about African

Larry Doby Was the Next

Hotels across the country refused to let [him stay]. He was denied service in restaurants. He was barred from entering ball parks in the South during spring training. . . . He was thrown at by opposing pitchers and spat on when he slid into base. He received hate mail from all over the country.[3]

This describes Larry Doby, the second African American to play Major League Baseball. On Saturday, July 5, 1947, about 11 weeks after Robinson joined the Dodgers, Doby took the field. An outfielder, Doby had been brought onto the American League's Cleveland Indians from a Negro leagues team, the Newark Eagles. He remembered feelings and experiences like Robinson's. The Indians' owner, Bill Veeck, had given Doby advice similar to that of Branch Rickey's:

No arguing with umpires, don't even turn around at a bad call at the plate, and no dissertations [arguing back and forth] with opposing players, either of those might start a race riot. . . . Remember to act in a way that you know people are watching you.[4]

Doby became a star on the field.

Americans' reactions in the stands.
Robinson wrote:

> Black support of the first black man in
> the majors was a complicated matter. . . .
> It was one thing for me out there on the
> playing field to be able to keep my cool in
> the face of insults. But it was another for
> all those black people sitting in the stands to
> keep from overreacting when they sensed a
> racial slur or an unjust decision. They could
> have blown the whole bit to hell by acting
> belligerently and touching off a race riot.
> That would have been all the bigots needed
> to set back the cause of progress of black
> men in sports another hundred years.[5]

Robinson later learned that the
African-American community held
meetings to discuss the importance of
acting civilly at the ball games.

Robinson did not play well during
the first game of the regular season
on April 15, 1947. He had no hits.
But soon he began to hit as well as he
had in Montreal.

Branch Rickey Meets with the African-American Community

Branch Rickey was concerned that African Americans might react with so much enthusiasm to Robinson that they would set back his acceptance into baseball. He met with leaders of the African-American community. He said:

Those 32 men organized all eight cities in the National League and did a beautiful job of it. And for two years not one of those things [that might create misunderstandings or increase opposition to Jack] was attempted or done.[6]

Robinson had been prepared for hate and abuse, but it was mild during the first few games. The Brooklyn fans seemed to love him, and fans and players from other teams were keeping quiet. But when the Philadelphia Phillies played the Dodgers, the Phillies' manager and several players shouted abusive comments, trying to make Robinson crack. He was strongly tempted to blow up and be done with everything. Robinson wrote:

> *I could throw down my bat, stride over to that Phillies dugout, grab one of those [white players] and smash his teeth in with my despised black fist. Then I could walk away from it all.* [7]

Instead, he thought of how many people were depending on him to keep cool. He especially thought of Branch Rickey deciding to bring up an African American and how much that might have cost him professionally and emotionally. Instead of giving in to his anger, Robinson used his expert base-running skills to score late in the game. That run won it for the Dodgers.

During the next two games, the Phillies expanded their comments to include the rest of the Dodgers. Finally, some of the Dodgers began to come to Robinson's defense.

Negative events continued that season, including a threatened strike by some players who did not want to play with Robinson. The baseball commissioner fought on Robinson's side and against the strike. He said any players who refused to play would be suspended.

Pee Wee Reese Supports Robinson

Later in the season, an event occurred that deeply affected Robinson. During a game in Boston, the fans and players were mocking Pee Wee Reese, the captain of the Dodgers. They said Reese, a southerner, should not play with an African American. During a break in the game, Reese walked onto the field and put his hand on Robinson's shoulder. The two men just talked; neither remembered later what was said. But the crowd got the message: Robinson was just a ballplayer, not an African-American ballplayer. The fans settled down, and the game went on. Reese later remembered thinking, "What he had to endure, the criticism, the catcalls—I wouldn't have had the courage."[8]

Jackie Robinson and Pee Wee Reese became close friends while playing for the Dodgers.

Reese and Robinson became good friends. While the Dodgers team continued to accept Robinson, hate mail and threats persisted. Some pitchers still tried to hit Robinson. Some base runners tried to injure him. Many fans and players shouted insults. Robinson often became angry, but he kept his promise not to react.

Rachel was especially supportive of her husband. She was the one person to whom he could talk about his true feelings. Without her, Robinson may not have been able to take the pressure of that first season.

The Dodgers went on to win the National League title. They played the New York Yankees in the World Series but lost in seven games. Robinson completed a superb year. He led the league with 29 stolen bases. He led the Dodgers in many categories. He received baseball's first Rookie of the Year award—even though he was far older than most other rookies who entered the majors that year.

Of that first season, Robinson said:

I had started off the season as a lonely man. . . . I ended it feeling like a member of a solid team. . . . All of us had learned something. I had learned how to exercise self-control. . . . My teammates had learned that it's not skin color but talent and ability that counts.[9]

Pee Wee and Jackie

Robinson always felt that Pee Wee Reese's show of support helped him overcome other players' and fans' dislike. On November 1, 2005, the city of New York unveiled a statue showing Reese with his hand on Robinson's shoulder. The statue is located outside the KeySpan Stadium, where the Brooklyn Cyclones play. The Cyclones are a minor league team associated with the New York Mets.

Jackie Robinson was a fast base runner and often led his team in stolen bases.

Jackie Robinson argued with an umpire before being ejected from a game for the first time in his career.

ON HIS OWN

During the 1948 season, Robinson began to look for ways to earn extra money. Robinson had lived on the league's minimum salary that season, even though his presence had boosted attendance for the Dodgers and other teams they played. So after Robinson's first season with the Dodgers, he was allowed to earn money outside of baseball. He began to use his influence to speak about civil rights issues.

Robinson had a slow start in the 1948 season. He had gained weight over the winter. He needed several weeks of hard work to return to his playing weight. It took him until about halfway through the season to lose the weight. He then began to look like the 1947 Robinson. By season's end, Robinson led the Dodgers in batting average, hits, doubles, triples, total bases, runs batted in, and runs scored. He was rated as the National League's best second baseman. He also led the league in the number of times he was hit by pitches.

BEING TREATED LIKE OTHER PLAYERS

There were indications that Robinson was making progress. Because of this, before the 1949 season Branch Rickey told Robinson, "Jackie, you're on your own now.

Ejected from the Game

Robinson said, "Not being able to fight back is a form of severe punishment."[1] After he got the okay from Rickey, he was able to act like any other player. During one game, he and his teammates were ridiculing an umpire who made a bad call. After the umpire's warning, all the players but Robinson stopped their comments. The umpire spun around and kicked Robinson out of the game. He later said, "He was treating me exactly as he would any ballplayer who got on his nerves. That made me feel great."[2]

You can be yourself again."[3] Robinson looked forward to acting like himself. He would not start trouble, but if it came, he would be able to face it.

By the 1949 season, Robinson was beginning to see other results from his sacrifices. Larry Doby, playing for the American League's Cleveland Indians, had become the second African American to enter the major leagues. By midseason, even more African Americans were playing. Robinson, Doby, Don Newcombe, and Roy Campanella all played in the 1949 All-Star Game.

Paul Robeson and HUAC

Paul Robeson was one of the most famous singers of the 1930s and 1940s. His fame became assured by his role in the musical *Showboat*. His version of "Old Man River" was famous nationwide. He lived for a time in Britain because of racist treatment he received in the United States.

Robeson became a supporter of communism. He believed it educated its people against racism. Back in the United States, Robeson publicly told young African Americans not to fight in any war against the Soviet Union.

The House Committee on Un-American Activities (HUAC) at this time was investigating artists such as Robeson. It believed most areas of the arts, government, and military were full of communist spies. HUAC asked Robinson to speak on Robeson's statements. Robinson agreed and flew to Washington DC. Robinson was clear that he did not support communism, but that Robeson had the right to express his views. After a riot at one of Robeson's appearances, Robinson said, "If Mr. Robeson wants to believe in Communism, that's his right."[4] He added that it was too bad that in the United States, "anything progressive is called Communism."[5]

The Dodgers played well that year. They won their league championship for the second time since Robinson had joined the team. In the World Series for the second time, the Dodgers lost once more to the Yankees. It was Robinson's best year with the Dodgers. He led the league in batting average. Robinson's outstanding play was recognized. He was voted the National League's most valuable player (MVP).

PUTTING DOWN ROOTS ON THE EAST COAST

In 1949, Robinson and Rachel moved with their young son, Jackie Jr., to St. Albans, near New York City. They had been living in a tiny apartment in Brooklyn during the baseball season. In the off-season, they lived in Los Angeles with family. Finally, they decided to settle on the East Coast. Not long after their move, on January 13, 1950, their

Roy Campanella

Roy Campanella was one of baseball's greatest catchers. He had been one of the players Rickey considered to be the first African American in Major League Baseball. Instead, he became the fourth. He joined the Dodgers in 1948. Robinson and Campanella did not always agree about the best way to integrate baseball. But both men were pioneers in their own ways. In January 1958, a car accident put Campanella in a wheelchair for the rest of his life.

The Robinson family in 1962. From left: Jackie, Sharon, David, Jackie Jr., and Rachel

second child, Sharon, was born. Their family expanded again in 1952 with the birth of their son David.

A Movie Star

During the 1950 season, Robinson's fame grew. He spoke to many groups and advertised many products. He also helped film his own life story in Hollywood. He played himself in *The Jackie Robinson Story*.

The season brought the departure of Branch Rickey. He and Dodgers chief legal counsel Walter O'Malley truly seemed to hate each other. O'Malley had wanted to control the Dodgers for some time. When one of the owners died, O'Malley bought his shares in the club. He also offered to buy Rickey's shares, but at a very low price. Rickey offered his shares to another investor for more money. To get the shares, O'Malley had to match the higher price. Rickey came away with $1 million, but his relationship with the club was finished.

Robinson wondered what would happen now. The question was answered when he signed a new contract for more money than ever before. But Robinson took Rickey's departure hard. Rickey had solidly supported Robinson no matter how bad things had been or how badly Robinson had played. In a letter to him, Robinson thanked Rickey for

A Family Man

Jackie Robinson loved his family, even though he often was away during the baseball season. He wrote them letters, telling them he missed them and was proud of them. Jackie and Rachel's love for each other also continued to grow. She kept him grounded, and he said she was "the one person who really kept me from throwing my hands up in despair many times." [6]

Jackie Robinson and Branch Rickey remained in contact after both retired from baseball.

helping him and all African Americans. Robinson and Rickey continued to have a close friendship until Rickey's death in 1965.

The next several seasons were both good and bad for Robinson and the Dodgers. On the last day of the 1951 season, Robinson hit a game-winning homer to get the Dodgers into the playoff series for the National League championship. But in the last game of the playoffs, the Giants beat the Dodgers and headed for the World Series.

In 1952, Robinson again led the team with great' hitting, fielding, and base running. The team made it to the World Series but again lost to the Yankees. In 1953, Robinson had another outstanding season, but again the Yankees defeated them in the World Series.

DODGERS, ROBINSON WIN COVETED WORLD SERIES

Finally, in 1955, the Dodgers won the World Series. That season and in 1956, Robinson had many injuries. He did not play as well as he had earlier in his career.

After the 1956 season, the Dodgers announced they would trade Robinson to the New York Giants. By the start of the 1958 season, both the Giants and the Dodgers would move to California. "[Jackie] was angry that the team to which he had been loyal hadn't even bothered to consult him on their plans to trade him," Sharon Robinson wrote.[7]

The Shot Heard Round the World

The American Revolutionary War (1775–1783) did not have the only "shot heard round the world." During the 1951 baseball season, the Dodgers were far ahead of their rival, the New York Giants. As the season went on, the Giants had a hot streak to tie the Dodgers by the last day of the season. The teams played a three-game series to see who would win the National League championship. The Dodgers led 4–2 in the ninth inning of the final game. Two Giants were on base. The Giants' Bobby Thomson stepped to the plate and blasted a home run to beat the Dodgers and win the series. The hit became known as "The Shot Heard Round the World."

Robinson had hoped to spend his entire career with the Dodgers. But he believed his best playing days were over and he was slowing down. He decided to retire but wanted to wait until he was ready to take another job before announcing the decision. Although angry, he publicly went along with the trade. Then, in the January 1957 issue of *Look* magazine, he made an official announcement. He was retiring. —

Jackie Robinson retired from baseball in 1957 after breaking the color barrier and playing in the major leagues for a decade.

Jackie Robinson worked as the vice president in charge of personnel at Chock full o'Nuts for seven years.

THE FINAL YEARS

When Robinson retired from baseball, he pursued other interests. He planned to work and to continue to help African Americans gain civil rights.

NEW BUSINESS VENTURES AWAIT

Bill Black, president of Chock full o'Nuts, a restaurant chain, offered Robinson a job as the vice president of personnel. He accepted. The Robinson children reacted to the news that their dad would come home from work every night: "As Dad prepared for life as a commuter, we imagined having him at home most nights in time for dinner. We liked the idea!" wrote Sharon Robinson.[1]

Around the same time, the National Association for the Advancement of Colored People (NAACP) asked Robinson to use his fame for its Freedom Fund Drive. Bill Black, although white, strongly supported the NAACP. Most of his employees were African-American. Black told Robinson he could use company time to travel and speak for the NAACP if it did not interfere with his Chock full o'Nuts work.

Robinson first came in contact with the NAACP when he was entering the major leagues. In June of 1956, Robinson had received an award from the organization. He was proud to receive the Spingarn Award, which had also been awarded to other famous African Americans such as W. E. B. Du Bois and Paul Robeson.

Robinson became a well-known speaker. At one church where he spoke, the audience stood and sang, "Jackie is our leader; we shall not be moved."[2] He pointed out that he believed the NAACP was good not only for African Americans but also for white Americans.

During the next year, Robinson traveled all over the country—Los Angeles, Boston, New York, Philadelphia, Miami, and Atlanta. In his first year as a fund-raiser, he helped raise more than $1 million for the NAACP.

Robinson and His Media

Robinson was always ready to use his influence to try to improve life for African Americans. He became a television commentator for a while. He had a radio show with NBC during the 1950s. He also wrote a newspaper column for the *New York Post* and other newspapers.

ROBINSON GETS INVOLVED IN POLITICS

Robinson became more active in politics. In the 1960 election, he supported the Republican candidate for president, Richard Nixon. Robinson believed Nixon's civil rights record as a U.S. senator was good. However, when Nixon would

Jackie Robinson played an active role in the NAACP and the civil rights movement.

not support Martin Luther King Jr., Robinson reconsidered his support. He continued to support Nixon but later said, "I do not consider my decision to back Richard Nixon . . . one of my finer ones."[3] Robinson also supported Nelson Rockefeller, the Republican governor of New York. Robinson resigned his position at Chock full o'Nuts to work with Rockefeller on civil rights.

One of Robinson's highest honors occurred in 1962. The Baseball Hall of Fame in Cooperstown, New York, honors the most outstanding players in baseball's history. Players must have been retired five years to be considered for membership. Robinson was chosen for this high honor in the first year he was eligible. He gave a brief speech on July 23. During his speech, he said that by receiving the award, "Everything is complete."[4]

Even during this honor, though, he was still thinking of how to help his fellow African Americans: "I think those of us who are fortunate, again, must use [their election to the Hall of Fame] in order to help others."[5] He was the first African American elected to the hall.

Robinson was not satisfied just to raise money to help African Americans indirectly. He decided he wanted to help more directly. With a group of business and community leaders, he helped open the Freedom National Bank on January 4, 1965. It was located in Harlem, a section

Jazz Afternoons

As part of his civil rights activities, Robinson was a fund-raiser. Among his other efforts, starting in 1963, he and Rachel hosted a series of jazz concerts in their home. They called the yearly event "An Afternoon of Jazz." Over the years, famous jazz musicians such as Dave Brubeck, Duke Ellington, and Dizzy Gillespie took part. Their first concert that summer raised approximately $15,000 for the Southern Christian Leadership Conference (SCLC). The concert series continues today through the Jackie Robinson Foundation.

of New York City populated mainly by African
Americans. The bank was owned and operated by
African Americans. It aimed to help Harlem and
the entire African-American community. Robinson
was chairman of the board until 1972. In 1970,
he established the Jackie Robinson Construction
Corporation.

LIFE-ALTERING EVENTS

In 1957, shortly
after he retired
from baseball,
Robinson was
diagnosed with
diabetes. This
blood disease
can lead to high
blood pressure,
blindness, and
death. By early
1972, he was almost
blind, and his legs
often hurt so badly
that walking was
painful.

Giving Back to the Community

Jackie founded the Jackie Robinson Construction Corporation with his friend and lawyer, Marty Edelman. It was established to build housing for lower income families and was an important enterprise for Jackie. Rachel later said, "Jack finally found the business opportunity he had been searching for since leaving baseball a decade earlier."[6] In 1970, work began on the Whitney Young Manor, the corporation's first development in Yonkers, New York, that would hold 197 apartments.

Edelman played a significant role in guiding his friend in the corporation. During this time, Jackie's health continued to deteriorate due to his diabetes. In 1968 and 1970, Jackie had mild heart attacks, and his vision continued to grow worse. Edelman worked to help keep the organization alive and his friend Jackie in the loop. He would call Jackie each evening to go over the day's events and make plans for the next day.

Another life-altering event occurred during Robinson's later years of life. In 1971, his son, Jackie Jr., died in a car accident. The Robinson family was deeply affected by this event.

On October 15, 1972, Robinson attended a World Series game. It was the twenty-fifth anniversary of his breaking the color barrier. Major League Baseball wanted to honor him. He was invited to throw out the ceremonial first pitch of the second game. He also made a short speech. During his speech, Robinson criticized the major leagues for not hiring any African-American managers. He was happy to be honored at the game, he said, but would be even more pleased "when I look at that third base coaching line one day and see a black face managing in baseball."[7]

Three years later, Robinson's wish came true. The Cleveland Indians hired Frank Robinson (no relation) as the first African-American baseball manager in 1975. Unfortunately, Jackie Robinson did not live to see the day.

About two weeks after his World Series appearance, Robinson collapsed at his home. He died on October 24, 1972, on the way to a hospital in Stamford, Connecticut. He was only 53 years old.

Robinson's death triggered a national outpouring of emotion around the United States. Former teammates, writers, politicians, and others paid tribute to him. Robinson's funeral service took place on October 29 at Riverside Church in New York City. More than 2,500 people attended the funeral. Many of his former Dodger teammates attended the service. The Reverend Jesse Jackson delivered the funeral address. He was a prominent civil rights figure and an associate of Martin Luther King Jr. Regarding Robinson's importance, Jackson said in part:

> *Jackie, as a figure in history, was a rock in the water, hitting concentric circles and ripples of new possibility. . . . There was strength and pride and power when the big rock hit the water, and concentric circles came forth and ripples of new possibility spread throughout the nation. . . . No grave can hold this body down. It belongs to the ages, and all of us are better off because the temple of God, the man with convictions, the man with a mission passed this way.*[8]

Five former teammates, including Pee Wee Reese and Don Newcombe, carried the casket from the church. After the service, the funeral procession left the church and headed for Brooklyn. Robinson was buried in Cypress Hills Cemetery, where his son, Jackie, was also buried.

After Robinson's death, Rachel began to take up the leadership of her late husband's businesses and organizations. She became president of the Jackie Robinson Construction Corporation, renaming it the Jackie Robinson Development Corporation. In 1973, she established the Jackie Robinson Foundation. She envisioned the foundation as a way to remember Jackie Robinson and his achievements, and as a means to grant scholarships to African-American students. The foundation has distributed more than 1,200 scholarships totaling more than $14 million.

Robinson continued to be honored after his death. On August 2, 1982, the U.S. Post Office issued a stamp picturing Robinson as a Dodgers ballplayer. On April 15, 1997, the fiftieth anniversary of Robinson's major league debut, Major League Baseball retired his number 42. No other Major League Baseball player will be allowed to wear the number. There is also a marker in every major

More than Scholarships

While a primary goal of the Jackie Robinson Foundation is to award scholarships to students, it is not the only mission of the organization. The foundation also serves as a resource for African-American students to develop and improve leadership skills by taking part in workshops, internships, and a mentoring program.

league ballpark commemorating Robinson's feat. In 2000, *Time* magazine named Robinson one of the 100 most important people of the twentieth century.

On October 29, 2003, the U.S. Congress awarded Robinson the Congressional Medal of Honor. This is the highest award the U.S. government can give someone outside the military. Congress said:

> *The legacy and personal achievements of Jackie Robinson, as an athlete, a business leader, and a citizen, have had a lasting and positive influence on the advancement of civil rights in the United States.* [9]

Robinson also changed the face of baseball. Years later, the participation of all races in all sports is unquestioned. Henry (Hank) Aaron, an African-American player for the Atlanta Braves, had the urging of a nation behind him as he chased Babe Ruth's career home run record in the early 1970s. Some racist pressure surfaced, but mostly, Americans wanted to see him break the record. Aaron broke Ruth's record, hitting his 715th home run on April 8, 1974. He ended his baseball career with 755 homers, a mark since surpassed by Barry Bonds.

More than a Baseball Hero

Robinson was a product of his times. He grew up as an African American in a divided nation. He bore the worst that racists could throw at him. But instead of lashing out in anger, he tried to open doors through word and example. He remained a gentleman on and off the playing field. Robinson will continue to be remembered as a contributor to the civil rights movement.

"A life is not important except in the impact it has on other lives."[10]

—carved on Robinson's gravestone

Robinson once said, "If you're going to spend your whole life in the grandstand just watching what goes on, in my opinion you're wasting your life."[11] Robinson lived by that statement. And because he did, he will always be remembered as a great baseball player and, perhaps more importantly, a great person.

Jackie Robinson broke the color barrier in baseball and paved the way for integration in all professional sports.

TIMELINE

1919	1920	1935
Jack Roosevelt Robinson is born on January 31.	Mallie Robinson moves her family to Pasadena, California.	Robinson starts school at Muir Technical High School.

1941	1942	1944
Robinson begins to play football for the Honolulu Bears.	Robinson enters the U.S. Army.	Robinson is arrested for not riding in the back of a military bus.

1937

Robinson begins
school at Pasadena
Junior College.

1939

Frank Robinson,
Jackie's brother,
dies in a motorcycle
accident.

1939

Robinson enters
UCLA.

1944

Robinson's army
court-martial begins
on August 2.

1945

Robinson plays his
first baseball game
for the Kansas City
Monarchs, a team in
the Negro leagues, on
May 6.

1945

Robinson and Branch
Rickey meet for the
first time on
August 28.

TIMELINE

1946

Robinson and Rachel Isum are married on February 10.

1947

Robinson becomes the first African American to play Major League Baseball in 60 years.

1949

Robinson receives the most valuable player award for the National League.

1971

Robinson's son Jackie Jr. dies in a car accident.

1972

Robinson makes his last public appearance, throwing the first pitch at the October 15 World Series game.

1972

Robinson dies in Stamford, Connecticut, on October 24.

1955

Robinson helps lead the Dodgers to the World Series title.

1957

Robinson retires from baseball in January. He takes a job with the Chock full o'Nuts restaurant chain.

1962

Robinson is elected to the Baseball Hall of Fame in Cooperstown, New York.

1982

The U.S. Post Office issues a postage stamp honoring Robinson.

1997

Robinson becomes the first and only player to have his number (42) retired by Major League Baseball.

2003

U.S. Congress awards Robinson the Congressional Medal of Honor.

ESSENTIAL FACTS

DATE OF BIRTH

January 31, 1919

PLACE OF BIRTH

Near Cairo, Georgia

PARENTS

Jerry and Mallie Robinson

EDUCATION

Pasadena public schools, Pasadena Junior College, University of California at Los Angeles (UCLA)

MARRIAGE

Rachel Isum, February 10, 1946

CHILDREN

Jack Jr. (born November 18, 1946), Sharon (born January 13, 1950), David (born May 14, 1952)

CAREER HIGHLIGHTS

Jackie Robinson became the first student to letter in four varsity sports at UCLA. He also became the first African American to play baseball in the major leagues.

SOCIETAL CONTRIBUTION

Robinson worked to gain equal rights for African Americans. He paved the way for African Americans in baseball and other professional sports. He labored for civil rights after retiring from baseball. Robinson raised more than $1 million for the NAACP. He also started a bank owned by African Americans and established a construction company to provide affordable housing for African Americans.

RESIDENCES

Cairo, Georgia; Pasadena, California; Brooklyn, New York; Stamford, Connecticut

CONFLICTS

Robinson stood up to unspoken but powerful segregation in the U.S. Army. As the first African American in professional baseball, he endured hatred and abuse from white fans and players in order to break baseball's "color line."

QUOTE

"If you're going to spend your whole life in the grandstand just watching what goes on, in my opinion you're wasting your life."
—*Jackie Robinson*

ADDITIONAL RESOURCES

SELECT BIBLIOGRAPHY

Jackie Robinson Foundation. <http://www.jackierobinson.org>.

Kahn, Roger. *The Boys of Summer.* New York: HarperPerennial, 1998.

Los Angeles Dodgers. "Jackie Robinson Timeline." <http://losangeles.dodgers.mlb.com/la/history/jackie_robinson_timeline/timeline_2.jsp>.

Rampersad, Arnold. *Jackie Robinson: A Biography.* New York: Ballantine, 1997.

Robinson, Jackie. *I Never Had It Made: An Autobiography.* New York: HarperCollins, 1995.

Robinson, Rachel, and Lee Daniels. *Jackie Robinson: An Intimate Portrait.* New York: Harry N. Abrams, 1996.

Robinson, Sharon. *Promises to Keep: How Jackie Robinson Changed America.* New York: Scholastic, 2004.

Tygiel, Jules. *Baseball's Great Experiment: Jackie Robinson and His Legacy.* New York: Oxford University Press, 1997.

FURTHER READING

Driscoll, Laura. *Negro Leagues All-Black Baseball.* New York: Grosset and Dunlap, 2002.

Eig, Jonathan. *Opening Day: The Story of Jackie Robinson's First Season.* New York: Simon & Schuster, 2007.

McKissack, Patricia C., and Frederick McKissack Jr. *Black Diamond: The Story of the Negro Baseball Leagues.* New York: Scholastic, 1994.

Web Links

To learn more about Jackie Robinson, visit ABDO Publishing Company online at **www.abdopublishing.com**. Web sites about Jackie Robinson are featured on our Book Links page. These links are routinely monitored and updated to provide the most current information available.

Places to Visit

Jackie Robinson and Pee Wee Reese Statue
KeySpan Park, 1904 Surf Avenue, Brooklyn, NY 11224
718 449 6368
www.brooklyncyclones.com
This statue commemorates the moment Pee Wee Reese walked onto the field and showed fans Robinson was a ballplayer to be respected. Watch the Brooklyn Cyclones play a baseball game at KeySpan Park after viewing the statue.

National Baseball Hall of Fame and Museum
25 Main Street, Cooperstown, NY 13326
800-425-5633
web.baseballhalloffame.org/index.jsp
Take a trip down baseball's memory lane at the National Baseball Hall of Fame and Museum. Be sure to check out an exhibition titled "Pride and Passion: The African-American Baseball Experience."

Negro Leagues Baseball Museum
1616 East Eighteenth Street, Kansas City, MO 64108-1610
816-221-1920
www.nlbm.com/s/index.cfm
Stroll through this museum and view many artifacts from the Negro leagues of baseball, including photographs, timelines, statues, and special exhibitions. A museum store is available to purchase books, clothing, and other baseball items.

GLOSSARY

barnstorming
　　Baseball teams playing in neutral locations in order to provide entertainment in cities that did not have their own teams.

civil rights
　　Personal rights guaranteed to all people by the U.S. Constitution and other acts of Congress.

civil rights movement
　　The struggle to gain equal rights for African Americans, especially during the late 1950s and early 1960s.

color line
　　An unwritten rule that kept African Americans from playing major league sports, including baseball and football.

commissioner
　　The administrative director of an athletic association.

court-martial
　　A trial of a military person that is conducted by a military court.

discrimination
　　Unfair treatment of people based on prejudice.

enterprise
　　A project that is undertaken for an important reason.

exhibition game
　　A game in which the teams play to develop skills and promote the sport rather than for a competitive advantage.

farm team
　　A minor league team that is controlled by a major league team.

honorable discharge
　　To leave the military before the end of duty with an honorable record.

Jim Crow laws
　　Customs and practices of unfair treatment of African Americans.

lynching
> The illegal hanging of someone, especially of African Americans by white Americans.

morale
> The spirit that unites a group toward a common goal.

Negro leagues
> Professional baseball teams for African Americans; the Negro leagues lasted from 1920 to the early 1960s.

personnel
> Employees of an organization.

pioneer
> A person who leads all others into new areas of thought or development.

plantation
> A large farm or estate that is farmed by people who live on the property.

prosecution
> The lawyers who represent the state during a trial.

protest
> To express strong objection to something, often done with a formal statement.

racism
> The unfair treatment of people based on race.

rookie
> A player in the first year on a sports team.

scout
> A baseball representative who looks for talented athletes to play for a team.

sharecropper
> A farmer who works for a landowner and gives the owner part of the crops that are grown.

SOURCE NOTES

Chapter 1. Breaking the Color Barrier
1. Arnold Rampersad. *Jackie Robinson: A Biography*. New York: Ballantine, 1997. 167.

Chapter 2. Life in Georgia
1. John A. Gable. "Roosevelt, Theodore." World Book Online Reference Center. 30 Oct. 2007 <http://worldbookonline.com/wb/Article?id=ar474860>.

Chapter 3. California and Its Challenges
1. Arnold Rampersad. *Jackie Robinson: A Biography*. New York: Ballantine, 1997. 53.
2. Ibid. 31.
3. Jackie Robinson. *I Never Had It Made: An Autobiography*. New York: HarperCollins, 1995. 9.
4. Arnold Rampersad. *Jackie Robinson: A Biography*. New York: Ballantine, 1997. 25.
5. Ibid. 39.
6. Jackie Robinson. *I Never Had It Made: An Autobiography*. New York: HarperCollins, 1995. 7.
7. Arnold Rampersad. *Jackie Robinson: A Biography*. New York: Ballantine, 1997. 27.
8. Timothy Kelley. "Stealing Hitler's Show." *New York Times Upfront*, 4 Sept. 2000. 32.

Chapter 4. Growing Up and Getting Out
1. Arnold Rampersad. *Jackie Robinson: A Biography*. New York: Ballantine, 1997. 49.
2. Ibid. 55.
3. Jackie Robinson. *I Never Had It Made: An Autobiography*. New York: HarperCollins, 1995. 11.
4. Arnold Rampersad. *Jackie Robinson: A Biography*. New York: Ballantine, 1997. 78.
5. Ibid. 78.
6. Jackie Robinson. *I Never Had It Made: An Autobiography*. New York: HarperCollins, 1995. 11.
7. Ibid. 12.

Chapter 5. Entering a World at War

1. Arnold Rampersad. *Jackie Robinson: A Biography*. New York: Ballantine, 1997. 44.
2. Ibid. 95.
3. Ibid. 112.

Chapter 6. The Negro Leagues

1. Arnold Rampersad. *Jackie Robinson: A Biography*. New York, 1997. 120.
2. Jackie Robinson. *I Never Had It Made: An Autobiography*. New York: HarperCollins, 1995. 25.
3. Ibid. 24-25.
4. Jules Tygiel. *Baseball's Great Experiment*. New York: Oxford University Press, 1983. 53.
5. Arnold Rampersad. *Jackie Robinson: A Biography*. New York: Ballantine, 1997. 122.
6. Ibid. 120.
7. Branch Rickey. *Branch Rickey Papers*. 17 Oct. 2007. <http://memory.loc.gov/ammem/collections/robinson/branch.html>.
8. Jackie Robinson. *I Never Had It Made: An Autobiography*. New York: HarperCollins, 1995. 33.
9. Arnold Rampersad. *Jackie Robinson: A Biography*. New York: Ballantine, 1997. 128.

Chapter 7. In the Minors

1. Jackie Robinson. *I Never Had It Made: An Autobiography*. New York: HarperCollins, 1995. 41.
2. Ibid. 48.
3. Arnold Rampersad. *Jackie Robinson: A Biography*. New York: Ballantine, 1997. 147.
4. Jackie Robinson. *I Never Had It Made: An Autobiography*. New York: HarperCollins, 1995. 52.

SOURCE NOTES CONTINUED

Chapter 8. Breaking into the Majors
1. Arnold Rampersad. *Jackie Robinson: A Biography*. New York: Ballantine, 1997. 164.
2. Ibid. 167.
3. Larry Doby. *Contemporary Black Biography*. Vol. 41. Gale, 2004. Biography Resource Center. Farmington Hills, Mich.: Thomson Gale, 2007. <http://0-galenet.galegroup.com.libraryapp. carverlib.org:80/servlet/BioRC>.
4. Ira Berkow. "He Crossed the Color Barrier, But in Another's Shadow." *New York Times*, 23 Feb. 1997. 1A.
5. Jackie Robinson. *I Never Had It Made: An Autobiography*. New York: HarperCollins, 1995. xxiii.
6. Branch Rickey. "Speech by Branch Rickey for the 'One Hundred Percent Wrong Club' banquet, Atlanta, Georgia. 20 Jan.1956. Broadcast on WERD AM radio." Oct. 31 2007 <http://memory. loc.gov/ammem/collections/robinson/branch.html>.
7. Jackie Robinson. *I Never Had It Made: An Autobiography*. New York: HarperCollins, 1995. 59.
8. Dave Kindred. "Jackie Robinson: One Man, Alone." *Sporting News* 14 Apr. 1997. 4 Aug. 2008 <http://www.sportingnews.com/ archives/jackie/kindred.html>.
9. Jackie Robinson. *I Never Had It Made: An Autobiography*. New York: HarperCollins, 1995. 68.

Chapter 9. On His Own
1. Jackie Robinson. *I Never Had It Made: An Autobiography*. New York: HarperCollins, 1995. 77.
2. Ibid. 75.
3. Ibid. 77.
4. Arnold Rampersad. *Jackie Robinson: A Biography*. New York: Ballantine, 1997. 216.
5. Ibid. 216.
6. Ibid. 199.
7. Sharon Robinson. *Promises to Keep: How Jackie Robinson Changed America*. New York: Scholastic, 2004. 51.

Chapter 10. The Final Years

1. Sharon Robinson. *Promises to Keep: How Jackie Robinson Changed America*. New York: Scholastic, 2004. 51.

2. Arnold Rampersad. *Jackie Robinson: A Biography*. New York: Ballantine, 1997. 317.

3. Jackie Robinson. *I Never Had It Made: An Autobiography*. New York: HarperCollins, 1995. 135.

4. Jackie Robinson. Pro Baseball Hall of Fame Induction Address. Found at American Rhetoric Online Speech Bank. 22 Oct. 2007 <http://www.americanrhetoric.com/speeches/jackierobinsonbaseballhofinduction.htm>.

5. Ibid.

6. Rachel Robinson and Lee Daniels. *Jackie Robinson: An Intimate Portrait*. New York: Harry N. Abrams, 1996. 208.

7. Arnold Rampersad. *Jackie Robinson: A Biography*. New York: Ballantine, 1997. 459.

8. Los Angeles Dodgers. "Jackie Robinson Timeline." 23 Oct. 2007 <http://losangeles.dodgers.mlb.com/la/history/jackie_robinson_timeline/timeline_2.jsp>.

9. 108th Congress. Public Law 108-101 (PL 108-101). 25 Oct. 2007 <http://frwebgate.access.gpo.gov/cgi-bin/getdoc.cgi?dbname=108_cong_public_laws&docid=f:publ101.108>.

10. Thomas R. Heitz. *Jackie Robinson*. Microsoft Encarta Online Encyclopedia 2008. 20 Jun 2008. <encarta.msn.com/encyclopedia_761574436/jackie_robinson.html>.

11. Peter G. Doumit. *What I Know About Baseball Is What I Know About Life*. Mustang, OK: Tate Publishing, 2007. 91.

INDEX

About the Author

Charles Pederson is a consulting editor, writer, and translator. He has written, or contributed to, many fiction and nonfiction publications for both children and adults. A graduate in linguistics, international relations, and German, he has traveled widely, bringing to his work an appreciation of different peoples and cultures. He lives with his family near Minneapolis, Minnesota.

Photo Credits